A Cat's
Night Before
Christmas

written by **Henry Beard**
created by **John Boswell**
illustrated by **Susann Ferris Jones**

A JOHN BOSWELL ASSOCIATES BOOK

BROADWAY BOOKS NEW YORK

'Twas the night before Christmas,
and all through the house,
Not a creature was stirring—
I'd killed the last mouse.

I awoke from a cat-nap and prowled through the place
For someone to play with or something to chase.

Tucked up in their bedrooms the humans all slept,
As out through the premises I casually crept.

From the edge of the mantel the stockings were hung
But a foot or two higher than I'd ever sprung.

They'd left out some cookies arranged on a plate
And a big glass of soy milk, a beverage I hate.

In a pot in the parlor, they'd propped up a pine,
A toy-laden scratching post that suited me fine.

But I'd already broken each low-hanging ball
And trashed any ornaments that happened to fall.

My cat-door was shut tight, the woodbin was stocked.
The plants had been brought in, the windows were locked.
On the lawn was that white stuff that freezes my paws;
I'll cough up fifty furballs before that stuff thaws.

The chipmunks were hiding in their smelly holes,
Rehearsing spring raids with the moles and the voles.

The last of the geese were flying off to Florida
To make some bum golf course a little bit horrider.

I could go dig my claws in the rare Persian rug,

And jiggle and jostle the frail Chinese jug,

And plop myself down on the off-limits chair,
But what is the point if there's nobody there?

To say I was bored 'twould be putting it mildly;
I was seized by a need to run around wildly.

I zoomed down the hallway—a world-record dash—
Then all of a sudden, I heard a slight crash.

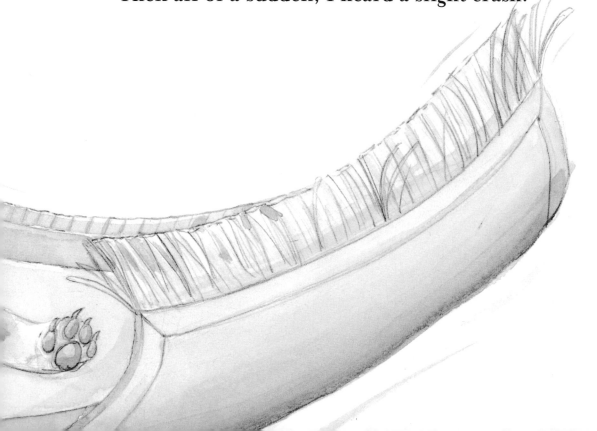

I may have brushed something
    left out on a shelf,
Though I think 'tis more likely
    it fell by itself.
The key to these mishaps
    is pure nonchalance—
A dignified retreat is
    the proper response.

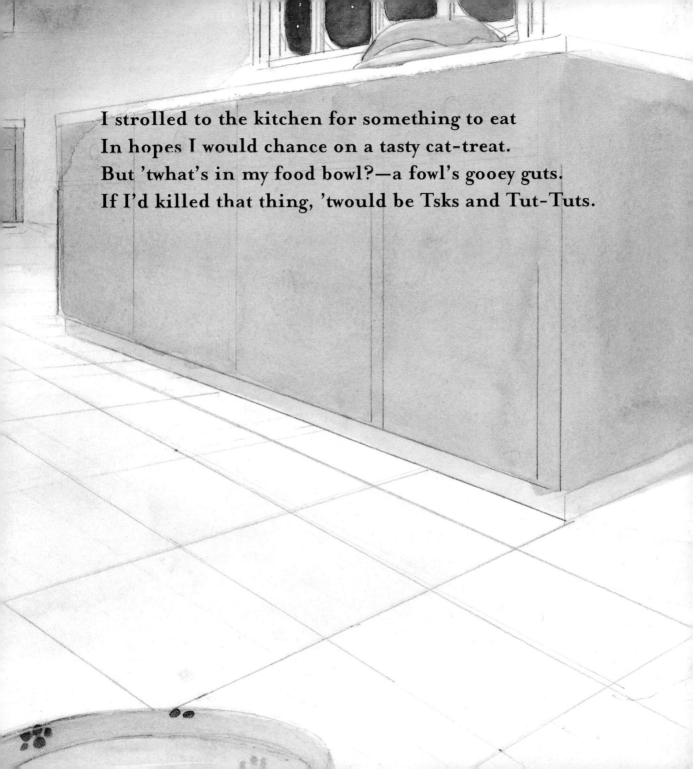

I strolled to the kitchen for something to eat
In hopes I would chance on a tasty cat-treat.
But 'twhat's in my food bowl?—a fowl's gooey guts.
If I'd killed that thing, 'twould be Tsks and Tut-Tuts.

On top of the counter, Birdzilla was thawing;
On that big ugly gobbler they soon would be gnawing.
I catch heck for nibbling a few baby sparrows
And they feast on turkeys the size of wheelbarrows.

I was starting to ponder how life is unfair
When just at that moment there came through the air
A conspicuous whiff of that marvelous herb,
An appetite for which no kitten can curb.

In the twitch of a whisker, off hunting I went
To track down the source of that tantalizing scent,

The telltale aroma—the potent perfume—
Of *Nepeta cataria*, oh luscious legume!

And there on the floor at the foot of the banister,
Its lid by its side, lay an overturned canister.

'Twas whatever it was that I just barely bumped,
And now on the parquet its contents were dumped.

'Twas a huge minty mound of delectable leaves—
Far better than mistletoe for cats' Christmas Eves.

And let me assure you no balsam or holly
Could make, on this holiday, yours truly so jolly.

I frisked and I frollicked—I quite lost my poise—
When from up on the roof beam there came a faint noise.

I pricked up my ears, and I heard a soft clunk,
Then a series of tip-taps and one final thunk.

I ran to the attic and stared through the skylight—
Had that feline elixir played tricks with my eyesight?

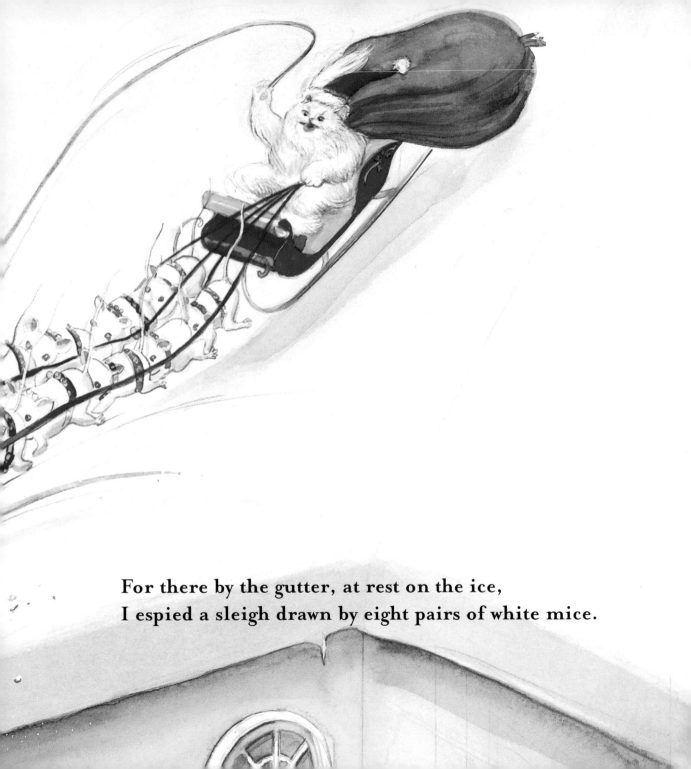

For there by the gutter, at rest on the ice,
I espied a sleigh drawn by eight pairs of white mice.

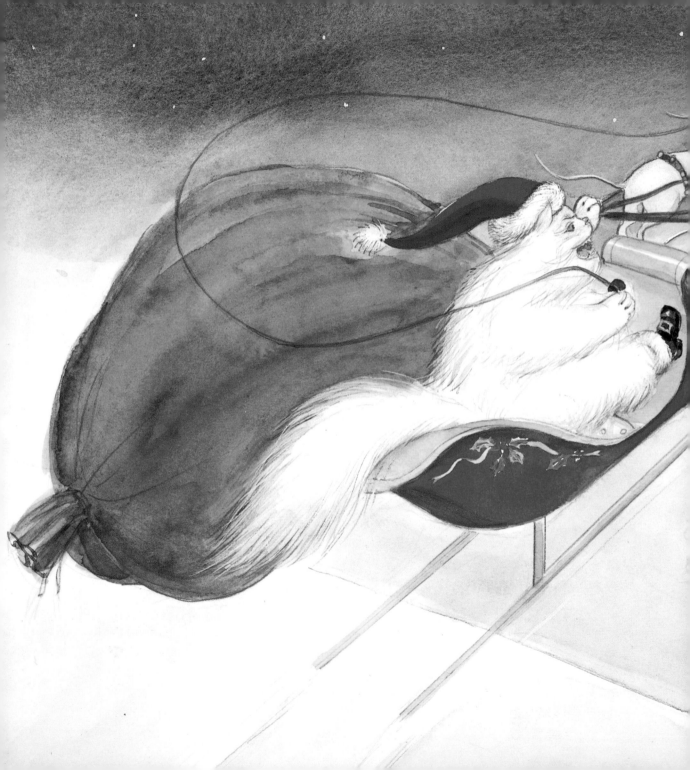

On top of the sled rode a plump silver cat,
With a bell-studded collar and a red Santa hat.
"*Get me off this darn roof*!" I heard him exclaim,
As he lashed at the rodents and called them by name.

"Down, *Dainty!* Down, *Scrumptious!*
Down, *Toothsome* and *Tasty!*
Down, *Morsel* and *Mouthful* and *Meatpie* and *Pasty!*"

"Down, *Juicy* and *Chewy* and *Yummy* and *Crunchy*!
Down, *Dumpling* and *Sushi* and *Nacho* and *Munchie*!"

When on *terra* much *firma* they safely alit,
He jumped from his perch, and I knew 'twas Saint Kitt.
His fur was alabaster, his booties were black,
And over his shoulder he lugged a huge sack.

The cat-door banged open—I heard him clomp in.
He clunked and he clattered and made quite a din.
As quick as a wink, down the stairs I did scoot—
But he'd hopped through the hatchway and left me his loot.

And there in the parlor, piled under the tree,
Were oodles of presents, and all just for me.
I dashed to the window and peered through the panes;
I watched him remount and take hold of the reins.

He mustered his scurriers and sat on his seat.
They squeaked and they chittered and stamped tiny feet.
And as they flew off with a crack of his rat-whip,

"Merry Christmas!" he called out, *"and lay off the catnip!"*

BROADWAY

A CAT'S NIGHT BEFORE CHRISTMAS. Copyright © 2005 by John Boswell Management, Inc. All rights reserved. No part of this book may be reproduced or transmitted in any form or by any means, electronic or mechanical, including photocopying, recording, or by any information storage and retrieval system, without written permission from the publisher. For information, address Broadway Books, a division of Random House, Inc.

PRINTED IN CHINA

BROADWAY BOOKS and its logo, a letter B bisected on the diagonal, are trademarks of Random House, Inc.

Visit our Web site at www.broadwaybooks.com

First edition published 2005

Book design by *Nan Jernigan*

LIBRARY OF CONGRESS CATALOGING-IN-PUBLICATION DATA
Beard, Henry.
A cat's night before Christmas / written by Henry Beard ; created by John Boswell ; illustrated by Susann Ferris Jones.
    p. cm.
    (alk. paper)
1. Cats—Juvenile poetry. 2. Christmas—Juvenile poetry. 3. Children's poetry, American. I. Jones, Susann Ferris. II. Title.

PS3552.E165C37 2005
811'.54—dc22

2005042122

ISBN 0-7679-1853-3

10 9 8 7 6 5 4 3 2 1